13-121

Law and Social Work

Statements prepared by

The National Conference of Lawyers and Social Workers

National Association of Social Workers, Inc.
1425 H Street, N.W.
Washington, D.C. 20005

NASW Pub. No.: ABL-060-C
ISBN: 0-87101-060-7
Library of Congress Catalog No.: 73-83804
Printed in the U.S.A.

Contents

Preface

THESE statements on subjects of special concern to members of the profession of law and the profession of social work were prepared by the National Conference of Lawyers and Social Workers, a joint committee of the American Bar Association and the National Association of Social Workers. Eight of the nine statements and the review in the appendix were previously issued as individual pamphlets, published from 1965 through 1969.

The same statements and the review appeared in various issues of the *Family Law Quarterly*, as follows:

"Rights of Public Assistance Recipients," Vol. 1, No. 1 (March 1967), pp. 72–81.

"Lawyer–Social Worker Relationships in Family Court Intake Process," Vol. 1, No. 1 (March 1967), pp. 81–85.

"Responsibilities and Reciprocal Relationships in Adoption—Lawyer and Social Worker," Vol. 1, No. 2 (June 1967), pp. 104–108.

"Legal Counsel for Voluntary Social Agencies," Vol. 1, No. 2 (June 1967), pp. 108–111.

"Adult Protective Services: Responsibilities and Reciprocal Relationships of the Lawyer and Social Worker," Vol. 2, No. 1 (March 1968), pp. 107–113.

"Lawyer–Social Worker Relationships in the Family Court Hearing and Disposition," Vol. 3, No. 1 (March 1969), pp. 49–53.

"Confidential and Privileged Communications: Guidelines for Lawyers and Social Workers," Vol. 3, No. 1 (March 1969), pp. 53–56.

"Interprofessional Relationships at the Graduate School Level: Law and Social Work," Vol. 4, No. 1 (March 1970), pp. 106–111.

"The National Conference of Lawyers and Social Workers: A Fifth Year Accounting" by Sol Morton Isaac, Vol. 1, No. 4 (December 1967), pp. 83–91. Reprinted in this booklet by permission.

MEMBERS OF THE CONFERENCE, 1973–1974

Representing the American Bar Association:
- Geoffrey G. Hazard, Jr., Co-Chairman
- Roy R. Barrera
- William M. Gibson
- Leonard V. Kaplan
- Sally Passette
- William E. Peterson
- Jerome J. Shestack
- Neva B. Talley

Representing the National Association of Social Workers:
- Bernard C. Fisher, Co-Chairman
- C. Wilson Anderson
- Earl J. Beatt
- Louis Bennett
- Leonel J. Castillo
- Mrs. Dolores Delahanty
- Genevieve T. Hill
- Walter L. Kindelsperger

Introduction

THE STATEMENTS collected in this publication were developed in the first decade of the National Conference of Lawyers and Social Workers. They were prepared as guides to practicing members of both professions as they encounter each other in the course of professional duties. Mainly the papers speak of proper assignment of tasks to the one or other practitioner; of distinctive yet complementary responsibilities to clients; and of relationships between members of the two occupations. One sees clearly that they are attempts to reduce abrasion on contact, increase harmony, and foster greater involvement of each with the other on matters of common concern.

In fact, these matters of natural interconnection and mutual interest between lawyers and social workers are legion and appear daily to grow in number and significance. Recognition of this led in 1962 to the creation of the Conference by the American Bar Association and the National Association of Social Workers. It is a joint committee, actually, of sixteen members, half appointed from each parent organization.

The Conference has been meeting about twice a year. What work has been accomplished has been done by the members themselves in and between meetings. With the one recent exception of the paper on child custody, these position papers were formally approved by the ruling bodies of both Associations. They were then widely distributed in a published series of pamphlets. Procedural changes in the Bar Association permit publication of the child custody statement on the decision of the Conference alone; the NASW Board of Directors continues to require its authorization.

The Conference has occupied itself, as charged, with "legitimate activities of social workers and lawyers in those areas where each has a vital interest." In years past the strong, abiding interest was in matters arising from the practice of family law. In addition to the papers assembled here, the Conference sought to encourage between local Bar and NASW units closer collaboration and common undertakings. It has welcomed opportunities to serve in consultative capacities to legal groups and social welfare organizations.

The Conference has changed, as everything alive must. It is now more a single body of like-minded members than a meeting of two self-conscious parties. Accordingly, problems in working relationships occupy it less; substantive issues in social justice engage it more.

The search of the Conference appears a consistent one of greater social and professional effectiveness of lawyers and social workers. The presumption then and now is that each strengthens the other through fellowship in common pursuit.

The merit of that notion is amply confirmed in the following statements.

Co-Chairmen:

Geoffrey G. Hazard, Jr.
for the American Bar Association

Bernard C. Fisher
for the National Association of Social Workers

1

Responsibilities and Reciprocal Relationships in Adoption—Lawyer and Social Worker

THIS STATEMENT is not designed to establish a comprehensive set of principles and practices pertaining to adoption and adoption procedures. Rather, it is intended to set forth the frame of reference within which lawyers and social workers may appropriately bring to bear their respective skills in discharging society's overriding obligation to protect the welfare of all children. Such broad legal-social principles as appear herein are illustrative of the reciprocal relationships and responsibilities of the two professions—law and social work.

RELEVANT CONSIDERATIONS

Relevant considerations that should prevail in adoption:

1. The placement of children for adoption should have as its main objective the well-being of children. The needs of the child should be paramount, with full recognition of the relevant needs and interests of the natural parents, adoptive parents, and society.

2. In addition to a framework of law that recognizes adoption as a method of establishing the legal relationship of parent and child between persons not so related at birth, the community or state provides adoption services through a duly organized, legally

controlled, and licensed social agency in or through which the several professions essential to a sound adoption service work together—law, social work, medicine. Social agencies are not generally involved in "relative adoptions," i.e., cases in which minor children are adopted by close relatives, including step-parents, except as called upon by the courts. Nonetheless, in all "relative adoptions" courts should obtain a social investigation as a condition precedent to approval of a petition of adoption.

3. Such an adoption service must be so organized that it affords the child, natural parents, and adoptive parents the help and protection that each must have:

a. The child should be protected from unnecessary separation from his parent(s) so long as they are capable of fulfilling, or may be expected with supportive service to fulfill, their parental role; from placement in a home that may be unsuitable or detrimental to his well-being; from intervention of natural parents after his placement in the adoptive home; and from loss of his right of a legal guardian of his person.

b. Parental rights of the natural parents should be safeguarded. They should be free from duress or undue pressure in making a decision about the child and should have the opportunity to consider alternative plans. They should not be reinvolved after legal relinquishment of the child and should have assurance of confidentiality.

c. A couple seeking to adopt children ought to be assured complete equity with others seeking children.

d. The adoptive parents should be protected through reasonable assurance by the adoption agency that the child is one for whom adoption is a suitable plan and that the placement is likely to be secure and stable. Moreover, they are entitled to the further assurance that the child is legally separated from his natural parents and that their identity is not known to the natural parents.

4. While recognizing that, in some jurisdictions, individuals, as such, may place or otherwise facilitate the adoption of minors, it should be emphasized nonetheless that social workers and lawyers, individually or jointly, when acting as individuals and not in cooperation with a qualified child placement agency, as aforesaid, do not have the facilities and resources necessary to provide protection and services needed by all persons affected by the adoption.

RECIPROCAL PROTECTION AND RIGHTS OF PARTIES

From the above it follows:

In recognition that adoption involves serious legal and social consequences, and that society quite properly insists on the highest degree of protection of, and consideration for, the rights, obligations, and responsibilities of all parties to the adoption—the child, the natural parents, and the adoptive parents—it is essential that all measures be taken to assure such reciprocal protection and consideration.

To this end, the respective parties are entitled to counsel of their own choice, through whom they may be advised of the *legal* consequences of their act and assured of the legality of the proceedings.

The attorney for the adoption agency, who may be either outside counsel or a full- or part-time staff member, represents essentially the interests of the child, in recognition of the in-loco-parentis role that his employer—the child placement agency—fulfills, and in further recognition of the legally sanctioned authority and responsibility that the agency assumes to safeguard, protect, and further the well-being of the child. It is not appropriate for the agency's counsel to represent all the parties to the adoption in regard to their respective legal rights, duties, and responsibilities.

In the application of the foregoing principles it is essential to take into consideration the following factors:

- Adoption, by and large, is not an adversary proceeding.
- Generally in an adoption, the legal obligations and responsibilities assumed by the adopting parents outweigh the rights relinquished by the natural parents.

LEGAL PRACTICES

With this in mind, it is suggested that the following considerations with respect to *legal* practices be observed:

1. Adoption agency counsel is responsible for assuring that the natural parent or parents as the case may be are advised, generally by the agency's social workers and through any written documents, that:

a. Legal consequences appertain to the surrender of their child or children for adoption and to the act of adoption.

b. The natural parent or parents may wish to consult with counsel of their own choice for the purpose of being *legally* advised in this regard.

c. If such parent or parents wish to avail themselves of independent counsel but either cannot afford to do so or do not have such counsel, the agency will make referral to the local Legal Aid Society or Bar Association referral service, as the case may be—assuming such a service exists in their community.

d. If the natural parents are unable to obtain independent counsel in the community, the social worker will suggest that in view of the fact that legal consequences attend the act of surrender, they should consult with the agency's counsel in this respect.

2. Upon surrender of the child for adoption, agency counsel is responsible for seeing to it that all legal requirements are met.

3. Agency counsel is responsible for seeing to it that the agency provides general information to adoptive parents about the legal duties and responsibilities they will assume, and about problems concerning rights of inheritance. However, because he recognizes that he cannot properly represent the natural parents, the child (the agency), and the adoptive parents, he makes certain that the adoptive parents are represented by counsel of their own choice. Together, agency counsel and the adoptive parents' counsel make certain that the adoptive parents fully understand the legal implications of the adoption, that statutory requirements are carefully followed through the placement and adoption proceedings, and that the preparation of the necessary pleadings and legal documents are such that the adoption decree, once granted, will be unassailable.

4. In all instances in which surrender is an involuntary act on the part of the natural parent or parents, agency counsel should recognize this as an adversary proceeding and should, through whatever means may be available to him and to the agency, see to it that the parent or parents are properly represented by independent legal counsel.

FUNCTION OF SOCIAL WORKER

The social worker's function is to:

1. Help the natural parents with the distinctive social and

emotional problems connected with considering the future of their child, including considering alternative plans as well as giving him up for adoption.

2. Provide any casework help related to the natural parents' own problems and possible need for rehabilitative help.

3. Help prospective adoptive parents who are seeking to adopt children determine whether adoption meets their needs.

4. Find and select adoptive couples and place children for adoption according to each child's particular needs and characteristics.

5. Provide interim care for the child, including study of the child in collaboration with professionals in other disciplines.

6. Provide assistance to the child and the adoptive parents during the period of adjustment between placement and legal adoption.

Both the lawyer and the social worker, jointly and severally, individually and through their respective professional associations and other appropriate bodies, have an obligation and responsibility to devote their skills and their efforts to an improvement of adoption laws, principles, practices and procedures, and agency and institutional facilities and resources so that society's concern for the well-being of the family may be reflected in the quality of community services provided in its behalf.

June 1965

2

Legal Counsel for Voluntary Social Agencies

THE AFFAIRS of most voluntary social agencies, like those of all other organizations, have become increasingly complex. Boards and administrative officers of many agencies—local, state, and national—find it necessary to seek legal advice on a wide variety of matters.

Broadly speaking, the occasions for seeking legal advice by most voluntary social agencies could be divided into four broad areas of agency concern:

1. Internal affairs, among which would be included:
   a. The structure and interpretation of agency organization.
   b. Staff employment and related problems.
   c. Taxation.
   d. Leases, property rights, and contracts.
   e. Insurance.
   f. Public (or private) liability.
   g. Fund raising, investments, and accountability.

2. Services affecting agency clientele, among which may be included:
   a. The extent to which social work counseling may encroach on the practice of law.
   b. Techniques for referring clients to lawyers or legal aid agencies.
   c. Cooperation with legal counsel for clients.
   d. Extent of confidentiality.

e. Aid to staff in the recognition of a situation that may have legal implications for a client or for clientele generally.

f. Extent of agency responsibility.

g. The agency in loco parentis.

3. The agency (or its staff) in court, among which may be included:

a. The agency as a litigant or in loco parentis.

b. The agency as a friend of the court.

c. Staff members as witnesses, voluntary or involuntary.

d. The court's appropriate utilization of the services of the agency.

4. The agency and the public, among which might be included:

a. The agency's active participation in public affairs, before the legislature, commissions, and other public bodies.

b. The agency's relations with the organized bar.

The foregoing illustrations are not intended to be all inclusive, since many agencies will have special problems while others will need legal advice less frequently. It is considered, however, that few if any agencies can afford to conduct their affairs without having some legal counsel available, even if only on an infrequent occasion.

Most voluntary social agencies do receive legal advice. This advice comes from either one of two or a combination of two sources: a member or members of the governing board or independently employed legal counsel. Some few large agencies may employ legal counsel as a part of staff.

It is certainly a fact that the vast majority of voluntary social agencies have at all times one or more lawyers as board members. It is generally true that these lawyer–board members contribute their competence, knowledge, and experience as lawyers to the deliberations of the board. Frequently, they are called upon to give legal advice to the agency and its staff in matters such as those enumerated above. Generally, this advice is given without charge. It is probably safe to say that this represents the way in which the majority of voluntary social agencies receive legal advice.

Without suggesting that the legal advice received by most voluntary social agencies is in the least inferior, the method described above has the following potential weaknesses:

• The lawyer–board members may be and usually are very busy lawyers who are contributing valuable time as board members and ought not to be expected to contribute more as lawyers per se.

• The lawyer–board members may have a limited term as board members and so the source of advice may change periodically.

• Legal advice is a valuable commodity. It ought to be paid for like medical advice, architects' fees, insurance premiums, and so forth.

The National Conference of Lawyers and Social Workers believes that every voluntary social agency should have competent and regular legal counsel and that such counsel generally ought not to be members of the agency's board. Since it is impossible to generalize beyond that statement for all voluntary social agencies, the Conference makes the following general suggestions:

1. That the board of directors of every voluntary social agency consider reasonable legal fees as an appropriate expense item for the agency.

2. That all federated funding groups and other resources that support voluntary social agencies consider reasonable legal fees as an appropriate expense item for these agencies. It is anticipated that, in most normal situations, lawyers in setting their charges would take into consideration the nature of the services.

3. That every voluntary social agency providing direct service to clients should receive legal advice concerning those areas of service that have legal implications or that might infringe on the practice of law.

4. That the agency's counsel, however he may be retained, should not undertake to counsel the agency's clients with respect to their legal rights and duties, and that the staff should not conclude that they can relate advice received from the agency's counsel to clients for the purpose of defining the clients' legal rights and duties.

June 1965

3

Rights of Public Assistance Recipients

One of the unique paradoxes of our modern industrial economy and of the affluent society it has fostered is the prevalence of poverty in the midst of plenty. Millions of men, women, and children in the United States are still living in poverty—below a minimum standard of health and decency.

Among these impoverished men, women, and children are the poorest of the poor, for whom public assistance payments constitute the only or primary source of income. Some are covered by the various categorical assistance programs established under the Social Security Act and administered by county, city, or State departments of public welfare, with Federal financial participation. They include the needy aged, the blind, the disabled, and dependent children. The remainder are beneficiaries of State and locally financed general assistance programs; some receive help from private philanthropy. Many more would be entitled to aid if actual need were the sole basis of eligibility.

THE CHANGING PATTERN OF MEETING SOCIAL WELFARE NEEDS

With the enactment of the Social Security Act of 1935—the first permanent legislation to authorize Federal financial aid to States for public welfare programs—a new pattern of meeting social welfare needs and a new set of Federal-State-local relationships emerged. This original enabling legislation, together with the various substantive amendments adopted in the 1950s and 1960s, gave recognition to the realization that in a highly complex and rapidly changing society, which was becoming increasingly mobile and interdependent, the need for a basic public program of social aid and services in every community in the Nation was an indispensable prerequisite to the provision of services to all who needed them.

The Social Security Act did not establish a Federally administered public welfare program to supplant existing State and local public welfare services. Rather, it provided Federal funds to stimulate State and local public welfare agencies to develop and enhance programs designed to alleviate poverty, prevent and reduce dependency, strengthen family life, deal with a wide range of individual problems, and contribute in a major way to the planning and organization of comprehensive community services.

Within this concept of Federal-State-local relationships and reflecting the fact that these programs were to be State administered or supervised, the Social Security Act contains relatively few requirements that States must meet in order to obtain this Federal aid. Despite the substantial and increasing share of public assistance costs paid from Federal funds, the definition of eligibility, amount of aid given, and—to a large extent—the scope and quality of public assistance and welfare services are matters for individual determination by each State government. And since all persons throughout the State defined as eligible must be treated alike, the amount of money available in relation to the need is a significant factor in the determination of the standards of aid and eligibility, with the ultimate authority on both counts residing in the same level of government.

FEDERAL REQUIREMENTS IN PUBLIC ASSISTANCE PROGRAMS

Regardless of the level of public assistance services that each State is free to determine without Federal direction or control, there are certain overall, specific requirements that are mandatory on all the States and that are relevant to the concern of the National Conference of Lawyers and Social Workers in its consideration of the rights of public assistance recipients.

These Federal requirements are based on principles that are fundamental to the achievement of the purposes and objectives of the public welfare titles of the Social Security Act. They reflect the most significant contribution that the enactment of this legislation made to the philosophy and concepts of public welfare: the concept that public assistance, however small the amount, is a legal right established by statute, legally enforceable, and subject to the same requirements of due process as are other legal rights. Assurance that State and local public welfare agencies will safeguard the basic rights of needy individuals in the administration of the public welfare program is required to be set forth in a State plan as a condition of Federal approval of the plan.

In addition to the general requirements that public welfare programs and benefits must be available statewide; that equitable, nondiscriminatory treatment must be accorded all individuals in like circumstances of need; and that services must be directed toward the attainment of self-support, self-care, and strengthened family life through the provision of essential preventive, protective, and rehabilitative services administered in a manner consistent with the protection of the dignity and self-respect of persons served; there are further specifications of individual rights. These include the rights of individuals to apply for assistance and, if eligible under the State plan, to be given financial assistance promptly and without discrimination; the right of individuals to be advised of the basis of a denial of assistance and the right to a fair hearing when aggrieved by the agency's decision; the right to receive money payments and the correlative right of choice in spending such funds free of agency control; assurance of confidentiality as provided by the Act and limitation of agency use of information concerning the recipient to uses that are required for purposes of administering the program. There is the further right to nondiscriminatory treatment under Title VI of the Civil Rights Act of 1964 as well as the general protection of fundamental constitutional rights.

RIGHTS IN LAW AND RIGHTS IN PRACTICE

Despite the statutory provision of individual substantive and procedural rights in respect to Federally aided public assistance programs, as well as the rights of the individual under the United States Constitution, it has become increasingly clear that these rights are not universally observed. It has also become evident that, covertly or overtly, individuals are being denied the protection of these rights and, indeed, perhaps the enjoyment of their basic constitutional rights as well.

Perhaps the most serious violations occur in agency practices about which precise information is lacking and difficult to obtain:

the low volume of fair hearings in some States and the implication that applicants and recipients have either not been adequately informed of this right to a fair hearing or discouraged from pursuing this remedy for their grievances, or that compromises or adjustments have been made on an informal basis to avoid the consequences of a formal hearing and the setting of precedents that would require altering agency policy or practice. Serious violations also occur in various intake practices, such as delaying or postponing interviews in order to discourage applications or using other means to deny assistance without taking an application; the use of pressure in regard to the manner in which recipients spend their assistance grants; and other agency practices in contravention of the State plan and written policies and procedures.

Some of the more dramatic instances of violation of individual rights occur in:

- Agency practices, policies, and procedures for determining eligibility that violate the right to privacy, e.g., "midnight raids."
- The attempt to control the behavior of parents by the denial of assistance to children, e.g., citing "conditions in the home."
- Work for relief enforced by criminal penalty.
- Provisions in State welfare laws regarding relatives' responsibility, in conflict with provisions of general law.
- Similar provisions with respect to residence requirements as a precondition for entitlement.

It should be noted, in this respect, that in the Social Security Act Amendments of 1965 establishing Title XIX, Congress has placed a limitation upon the States in the medical assistance program. The State may not impose responsibility for support of a relative other than a spouse or child under 21 and may not have a residence requirement that excludes a resident of the State.

These and related issues raise questions related not only to individual rights established in public welfare statutes but also to basic questions of constitutional law and matters involving administrative agency practices and procedures—all of which are within the unique competence of lawyers. Of further significance and importance are laws and practices respecting general as distinguished from categorical assistance programs, in which there is no Federal financial participation and to which Federal public assistance statutes do not apply. The need is no less imperative for those denied the protection of relevant Federal welfare laws, who nevertheless enjoy basic constitutional rights and the protection afforded in many jurisdictions by relevant State laws.

Until relatively recently there has been little critical examination of the issues of substantive law and procedure inherent in public welfare statutes and agency practices. Legal representation involving the traditional advocacy or adversary role of lawyers in the field of public welfare has been virtually nonexistent. Indeed, the very extent of the legal rights accorded those whose condition in life compels them to seek public assistance has had neither the benefit of extensive legal research nor the binding or persuasive value of precedents established by test cases—the traditional way in which law evolves and renews itself. Nor has there been any critical examination of the policies and practices of public welfare agencies or of the statutes and regulations from which they presume to take sustenance.

The effectuation of the right of entitlement is the function of the lawyer and legal institutions. Rights of public assistance applicants are not self-executing; these individuals are often unaware of their rights and almost always lack legal counsel to represent them in their efforts to obtain the rights they are entitled to by law.

Despite the efforts of outstanding members of the legal profession in respect to the safeguarding and effectuation of the rights of public assistance applicants and recipients, it is generally recognized that lawyers have not been formally trained for service in this area, nor have the agencies or individuals concerned generally considered it to be an area requiring legal skill and competence—even assuming the availability of lawyers to provide help when needed. Thus, decision-making with respect to fundamental human rights has rested essentially with public welfare officials and staff.

The law and the legal profession have historically served as guardians of human rights, freedoms, and liberties. The effective enforcement of the right of entitlement established by law and the free and untrammeled exercise of the rights all individuals—rich and poor alike—have under the Constitution present a challenge to the Bar and to all concerned with the sanctity of the rule of law. The concept of legal entitlement, which is at the heart of our public welfare laws today, can have no meaning, no validity, if in practice it is violated or ignored with little fear of adverse consequences. Thus the rule of law and the cherished protection of due process become a mockery to those who are the most disadvantaged, the most defenseless, the most vulnerable, and the most needy. Without the active intervention of the Bar and the availability of legal services to assure equitable enforcement of the law, the intent and meaning and purpose of the rights established under the Social

Security Act are without value, and the law as well as a democratic society is demeaned thereby.

RELATED LEGAL NEEDS OF PUBLIC ASSISTANCE RECIPIENTS

Involvement of the legal profession in the area of public welfare law is a natural extension of its traditional concern for human rights. It is also a logical next step for a profession that has met the challenge of legal representation for the indigent accused and has resolved to deploy its resources in the nationwide War on Poverty. There is evidence of much interest and concern both in professional associations and law schools and a growing awareness of the contribution to be made by the legal profession in a variety of ways to the goal of assuring social justice for all persons.

The legal problems of public assistance applicants and recipients are myriad and extend beyond the protection of their rights in relation to the public welfare agency. These poorest of the poor are generally deprived, poorly educated, uninformed as to the law, often compelled to purchase on credit, and often entangled in complicated marital and family relationships. They are typically the victims of unscrupulous and incompetent purveyors of unauthorized legal advice—are in great need of legal counsel and representation in situations involving credit, eviction, domestic relations problems, denial of access to public housing, and related matters. Legal services are often as essential and helpful in the total rehabilitation process as are social services and financial aid.

The quality of justice must be measured by the extent to which all who are in need have access to legal services as and when required. Society as a whole has the obligation to contribute to the provision of required legal services by giving suitable financial assistance and furthering the efforts of the organized Bar and other appropriate groups. An American Bar Association resolution of February 8, 1965, expressed this obligation for

> . . . the development and implementation of programs for expanding availability of legal services to indigents and persons of low income, such programs to utilize to the maximum extent deemed feasible the experience and facilities of the organized bar, such as legal aid, legal defender, and lawyer referral, and such legal services to be performed by lawyers in accordance with ethical standards of the legal profession.

Recent activities by the American Bar Association and the National Legal Aid and Defender Association that relate to the organization and provision of legal services to the poor include the following: efforts supporting the establishment of new legal service programs, organization of university-sponsored research and study centers, revision of law school curricula, and provision of legal services by selected law students under appropriate authority and qualified supervision. These are indications of the extent of the legal profession's commitment to its role in the War on Poverty.

The interest of governmental agencies, public welfare agency administrators, and the social work profession is further evidence of the commitment of these official and voluntary agencies to the common goal of providing legal services to all who need them. Increased support of legal aid services in many communities also foreshadows enhanced legal protection through an institution that has functioned in this area for almost a century.

GUIDELINES FOR THE PROFESSIONS

Social workers and lawyers have primary functions to fulfill in serving the needy. Both groups must work cooperatively to:

- Identify needs requiring their individual or joint professional competencies.
- Help to resolve situations that involve both social and legal problems—which includes recognizing and reconciling their respective professional orientations, especially as related to the adversary role.
- Develop machinery and procedures for effective referral relationships.
- Keep continuously informed as to available social and legal resources and plan in concert with other groups to organize, develop, and expand services as required.
- In keeping with their respective professional authority and responsibility, help to assure the provision of preventive legal service—including educational programs designed to help individuals become more aware that they need legal services and that such services are available.
- Help to assure effective realization of the right to a fair hearing in public welfare proceedings and bring to light agency policies, procedures, and practices that do violation to the right of individuals and operate to the detriment of applicants and recipients of public assistance.

• Engage in a systematic, thorough, comprehensive survey of the rights of clients of the public welfare department and their evaluation in relation to the agency's policies, practices, and procedures, with special emphasis on the extent to which recipients are helped to live in dignity and achieve the goal of maximum self-support and independence.

• Encourage the public welfare agency to pay for lawyers' fees for representation at fair hearings, with the client having the right to free choice of legal counsel or the use of lawyer referral services and with appropriate fee schedules determined in agreement with local Bar organizations.

• In collaboration with schools of social work and schools of law, help to forward and promote curriculum development, research and survey activities, fieldwork and continuing education, and related matters.

• Insure the elimination of unqualified and unlicensed persons from the ranks of those serving the legal or counseling needs of the poor.

• Explore the role of voluntary nonprofit social agencies in respect to the provision of legal services to the poor, including the role and responsibility of community councils and related health and social planning bodies in supporting, as appropriate, legal processes deemed essential to assure effectuation of rights of welfare assistance applicants and recipients.

There is no single answer and no single national pattern emerging that makes meaningful the promise of equal justice under law for all—including the poor who are the primary object of our concern. Progress may be anticipated through the following: experimentation, the growth of new and continuing patterns of cooperation between the law and social work, and the development of new forms of organization that are consistent with the requirements of professional ethics for providing services to the poor, as well as new techniques and improved methods for doing so. All these offer unparalleled opportunity for innovation and close collaboration between the two professional disciplines—law and social work—most vitally concerned in this area of common interest and shared responsibility.

If the objectives sought are to be realized, it is crucially important that lawyers and social workers—including public welfare officials—meet together at the local level with governmental representatives of appropriate governmental and voluntary organizations and, as suitable, representatives of the poor themselves to analyze the problem of availability of legal services for public assistance applicants and recipients and the poor generally. Their discussion might include the extent of the need for such services in relation to existing traditional legal aid and related services. They might also plan when necessary for the provision of needed services, considering auspices, organizational structure, location or locations, financing, and study and evaluation.

In the final analysis the task must be performed locally, where the people are and where the services should be. This places the primary burden on the local community, its legal institutions and social agencies, and its resident lawyers and social workers.

January 1967

4

Lawyer–Social Worker Relationships in the Family Court Intake Process

The juvenile court originated in 1899. It constituted a departure from the conventional adversary process of the criminal court and advanced the concept of "individualized" justice for juveniles, through a judicial inquiry. Under the principles of parens patriae or in loco parentis the juvenile court assumed the task of protecting the child from himself, protecting the community, and rehabilitating the child.

Family courts for the adjudication of family-centered problems have been founded along the same general lines as juvenile courts but are not nearly so widespread. The juvenile court generally deals with delinquency, dependency, and neglect and has jurisdiction as well over some other situations relating to children, such as adoption and custody. The concept of the family court is beginning to embody the philosophy, procedures, and jurisdiction of the juvenile court and to extend them. They are being applied to matrimonial actions, paternity proceedings, and criminal actions involving relationships between members of the same family, such as assault on a spouse, nonsupport, desertion, and contributing to the neglect or delinquency of children. Many family courts include juvenile matters, and "family court" as used in this publication includes them. In these courts, the protective role of the court extends to the family as a basic unit of society and seeks to preserve or restore it as a socially functioning and law-abiding unit.

Various interpretations of the underlying statutes picture the family courts as administrative agencies, social courts, and chancery courts and use other terms that tend to de-emphasize the purely legal aspects of the judicial process. Often these interpretations obscure the legal rights of children and families, disregard or minimize due process, and ignore the necessity of establishing a basis in law and in fact for official intervention in the lives of people.

Other interpretations of such statutes liken the family courts to criminal courts, tending to ascribe to them an overly formal, legalistic, and adversary approach. The view tends to ignore the immaturity of children, the need to provide enlightened corrective help, and the emotional problems frequently involved in family matters. Such a view may serve to widen the breach among members of a family suffering internal conflict and emotional stress.

The concept of courts as sociolegal institutions has experienced a unique development in family courts. Here some of the functions of social workers and lawyers are different from their roles in other courts. The participation of social workers is more significant than in other courts where their function is limited primarily to social investigation. To some extent, the role of the lawyer is changed in the family courts where there is more informality and flexibility in procedure and disposition. It is, therefore, highly desirable for lawyers and social workers to define those concepts that are believed basic to their working relationships to one another in these courts.

This statement recognizes that the consolidation of the full range of family problems within the jurisdiction of a single court has not been accomplished on a broad scale. It does not consider the merits of such consolidation. It also recognizes that some of the so-called family courts have not, in fact, changed in operation or philosophy but only in name. Modification of law or procedure in these aspects is likewise outside the scope of the statement. It is further limited to relationships involved in the intake process.

In all courts there are established procedures for initiating court action. Usually these procedures are routine and are concerned with the accurate recording of claims, statements, or legal documents required for the matter to come before the court. These procedures are steps in the legal process of initiating a specific court action and do not involve an exploration of the possibilities of nonjudicial resolution of the problems.

The concept of intake as a step preliminary to legal process is relatively unknown to the law except in juvenile and family courts. When intake procedures exist, they have been created either by legislation or court rule. It is to the advantage of many people to have help in exploring the possibilities of a nonjudicial resolution of their problems. To provide this help, personnel have been hired who are on the staff of or responsible to the court. The service has been largely in the hands of social work personnel and not in the hands of lawyers, prosecutors, or others trained in the legal process. *The chief function that these personnel perform is helping litigants recognize when it might be more effective to accept appropriate treatment services* rather than invoke the judicial process. However, the intake workers should never prevent or inhibit the application of the judicial process in any case or situation. It must be remembered that no one can foreclose the rights of any individual to pursue his remedies in court if he desires to do so and that there must be compliance with the provisions of law and full protection of the legal rights of all parties.

GUIDING PRINCIPLES

It is hoped that the following principles will guide the relationship of the lawyer and the social worker in whatever court to which family and juvenile problems are brought:

1. The judicial nature of the court as an ultimate resource should at all times be kept in mind. Its operations are legal and involve involuntary proceedings as far as the defendant is concerned.
2. The intake service should evaluate which cases might be adjusted without resort to formal judicial proceedings and, when appropriate, attempt to adjust such cases through social investigation and counseling, either using its own resources or referring the cases to other community services.
3. Appropriate social services should be available to persons involved in various phases of family problems, including full use of community resources when it is clear that help can better be given out of court and this alternative is mutually agreeable.
4. All participants—lawyers, social workers, and judges—should be dedicated to working toward the best interests of the individuals and families concerned. Lawyers should recognize that they do not have the specialized training and experience in social casework that may be needed to handle certain social problems. Likewise, social workers should recognize that they do not have legal

training and are not authorized to practice law or make determinations of a legal nature.

In family court intake, the lawyer and the social worker share a common goal in relation to the interested parties. The social worker is on the staff of or responsible to the court, the lawyer is an officer of the court, and both should be equally concerned with the rights and the interests of the parties. These rights and interests may be protected best by resolving the conflicts through cooperative efforts upon consent of the parties rather than by routine scheduling of a hearing before the judge. Such a hearing should not be denied when requested. Lawyers and social workers, however, should unite in efforts to explore thoroughly whether or not more appropriate help might be supplied without the application of the judicial process. This may include referral to other agencies or resources.

With these concepts in mind, the following roles are appropriate:

ROLE OF THE SOCIAL WORKER

The court intake worker, in assessing whether or not a voluntary adjustment without a judicial hearing is appropriate, should:

1. Consider whether the alleged facts appear to represent a case coming within the purview of the court.

2. Make certain that the parties are appropriately informed of their right to legal counsel and right to a court hearing and that they are assisted in obtaining such counsel if desired.

3. Explore with the lawyers the need for judicial as well as alternate measures that may offer mutually acceptable solutions to the problem.

4. Respect the confidentiality of information disclosed by the client and the lawyer, cooperate as fully as possible with the lawyers, and share with them pertinent information bearing on the intake plan.

ROLE OF THE LAWYER

The lawyer representing clients at intake in family matters should:

1. Provide legal advice to his client and assist the intake worker to interpret to the client the functions, aims, and limitations of the family court.

2. Participate in the intake decision-making process, sharing

with the intake worker pertinent nonconfidential information and assisting his client to understand and accept the most beneficial decision.

3. Respect the confidentiality of information disclosed by the client and by the social worker.

Lawyers have a function other than as contestants in adversary proceedings. They are officers of the court and counselors-at-law as well as advocates for the best interests of their clients. Neither the court nor the court-attached social worker should discourage participation of independent counsel for all parties in family and juvenile court matters. On the other hand, they should encourage consultation with a lawyer. Lawyers should recognize the value of and encourage the use of social resources for the welfare of the clients. Both lawyers and social workers should discharge their responsibilities in such a manner as to prevent or lessen hostilities and promote respect for the authority of law and the administration of justice.

January 1967

5

Adult Protective Services—Responsibilities and Reciprocal Relationships of the Lawyer and Social Worker

One of the most significant phenomena of the times has been the unprecedented increase in the number and proportion of older adults in our population and society's growing interest and concern for their well-being. Although many persons of all ages find that coping with the increasingly complex problems of everyday life presents a hazard they are unable to surmount, it is recognized that among the aged—as well as the retarded, the alcoholic, and the addicted—there are many who suffer additional disabilities that impair their daily functioning.

These disabilities—physical, emotional, mental—vary from person to person, and the individuals involved range from those who are a danger to the community to those unable to manage some of their affairs. The degree of disability may also vary from day to day; for some there is steady deterioration, for others there is fluctuation.

Increasingly, lawyers and social workers are faced with the need to deal with the myriad personal problems associated with older persons who do not seem to be able to participate responsibly in making decisions concerning their own welfare. They must deal with those who are disoriented, who do not remember what they did with their funds and belongings, who cannot remain rooted and are constantly moving from place to place, who persist in remaining in admittedly dangerous living accommodations, or who live in seclusion and refuse proffered help.

Recourse to traditional community health and social services and traditional forms of fiduciary arrangements often proves helpful in some of these situations. Our concern here is with the growing number of adults who are so limited in functional capacity that even with supportive help, they require some kind of formal intervention for their own and society's protection. The means must be provided by which assistance may be rendered to these persons to the end that they may remain in the community as long as possible, living as full lives as possible. When this is no longer feasible, appropriate institutional facilities must be provided to care for them. Assistance must also be rendered so that others like them may be returned to the community from the institutions in which they are now to be found.

In considering a solution to these problems it is imperative to acknowledge the right—inherent in a democratic society and a matter of deep tradition in the United States—of each individual to be free to make his own decisions about his life. This right, however, is tempered by the basic right of any society to take appropriate steps to protect its peace and security. This "police power" also imposes on that society an obligation to assist those unable to manage for themselves, in order that the peace and security not be disturbed. The legal doctrine of parens patriae is the humanitarian notion that describes the responsibility of the state as a guardian of the weak. The combination of these principles requires that intervention be undertaken only in clearly indicated circumstances under procedures designed to protect the individual's freedom.

The services necessary to assist these persons are generally called "protective services." They are defined as those activities undertaken by an individual or agency on behalf of certain recognizably incapable or incompetent persons, which have as their goal the placement or care, or both, of these persons under some form of legal authority for their own or others' protection.

GENERAL OBSERVATIONS

A protective-service program involves the participation and contribution of many professions. Principal among them are medicine, psychiatry, law, and social work, each with its own unique and distinct function to fulfill and all with mutual, interrelated, and complementary responsibilities. These functions and responsibilities derive from the nature of these professional disciplines and their respective orientation and value systems. They also stem from the ethical commitment of members of the professions to respond to society's obligation to use their judgment, competence, and authority to intervene and protect those persons whose capacity to make responsible decisions in their own behalf in crucial areas of their lives is so lacking as to constitute a danger to themselves or society.

Each of these professions reflects in practice common convictions about the worth and dignity of the individual, his rights and liberties, freedom to make his own choices and his own decisions, and his right to live his own life in his own way—no matter how bizarre or unconventional—as long as his behavior does not unduly imperil his own life or threaten society. Similarly, each must understand and be prepared to intervene when conditions indicate the imperative need to do so.

While recognizing that protective service—involving as it does an act of intervention under the color of legal authority—must be based on law, it must also be acknowledged that in the absence of an interrelated program and network of essential preventive, supportive, and rehabilitative services and facilities, the law that confers the authority to act for and on behalf of an incapacitated person is of limited value and significance. For indeed, both services and law—supported by appropriate structure, requisite personnel, and adequate funding—are the essential components of a good community protective-service program.

FUNCTION OF THE SOCIAL WORKER

Social work—social casework in particular—is at the core of a good protective-service program. The professional social worker makes his contribution to the provision and administration of protective services through his:

- Understanding of the life cycle of the individual and the aging process and its effects on the individual.
- Knowledge and understanding of relevant therapeutic techniques.
- Expertise in psychosocial diagnosis, including evaluation of the individual's potential for social functioning.
- Participation in the development of adequate treatment plans, including decisions as to placement.
- Creative use of appropriate community resources, as required, and skill in community planning.
- Provision of direct and ancillary services, often through the remainder of an older person's life, at any time of the night or day.

In performing these functions, the social worker is called upon to:

• Help incapacitated persons cope with their disabilities by maximizing their remaining capacities and resources and enhancing their potential for social functioning in the community.

• Recognize the need for medical and psychiatric treatment services, including temporary screening facilities for diagnostic evaluation and development of adequate treatment plans.

• Identify specific needs of the incapacitated and further the development of resources designed to help these persons remain in or return to the community. These needs and resources include adequate public assistance programs related to income maintenance, social services, medical care and legal services, family service agency programs, housing, educational and recreational programs, rehabilitation and employment services, special services such as some health care, foster family placement, and related services.

• Further the provision of flexible placement procedures and alternatives. This encompasses continual review of need and review of appropriate institutional facilities that are available as required for incapacitated persons who even with adequate supportive services cannot remain in the community—including hospitals, nursing homes, homes for the aged, and the availability of casework and related services in these facilities.

• Engage in case-finding activities and reach out to provide early treatment and service, especially in respect to persons who are without family or close friends, withdrawn, and isolated.

• Distinguish between incompetency proceedings and hospitalization proceedings and understand that a legal finding of incompetency is not a prerequisite to hospitalization or its inevitable result in many jurisdictions.

• Be alert to the need to invoke legal sanction and to understand the contribution the law can make in protective services, especially when there is a need to take emergency action and time does not permit ordinary recourse to court orders.

• Participate in the establishment of cooperative consultative referral and reporting relationships.

FUNCTION OF THE LAWYER

The law is the base upon which an effective protective-service program must rest. The lawyer contributes to the provision and administration of protective services through his:

• Knowledge of the law: its genesis, growth, and development; its goals and objectives; its continuing evolutionary process; its role and function in contemporary society.

• Knowledge of the essential legal considerations that relate to incapacity and the legal problems resulting therefrom, including such matters as determination of disability, hospitalization and release, personal and property rights and status, and related legal matters.

• Knowledge of the requirements for law-making and the problems involved in incorporating into substantive law and practice advances in sociomedical knowledge; continuous study and observation of the working of the law to assure its adequacy in coping with the problems of incapacity as well as the advances in knowledge.

• Expertise in legal and judicial procedures and techniques.

• Understanding of institutional and governmental structure, and legislative and administrative practices.

• Provision of representative and consultative legal service.

The lawyer's responsibility requires that he:

• Represent alleged incapacitated persons to prevent undue infringement of rights and to enhance those rights.

• Advise other professionals of the legal implications of proposed courses of action.

• Assist in the development and execution of plans for incapacitated adults to assure compliance with the law. This includes, when appropriate, legal instruments of trust, power of attorney, and other fiduciary arrangements.

• Represent those who seek the legal authority necessary to provide services to the incapacitated.

• Further the development of legal services for incapacitated persons unable to afford private counsel and the development of adjunctive services to assist courts and guardians, trustees, conservators, or similar persons in the performance of their responsibilities.

• Assure effectuation of the right of alleged incapacitated persons to confidentiality.

• Further the establishment of procedures for continuing review of actions taken by guardians and custodial authorities to assure accountability; also the establishment of periodic and timely review to determine whether the conditions and circumstances that led to legal intervention still prevail.

• Adapt the use of traditional adversary techniques to conform to the special needs of this problem.

• Recognize the need for medical, psychiatric, and social work services and understand their contributions to the incapacitated person as well as the need for cooperative working relationships.

JOINT RESPONSIBILITIES

Many agencies and organizations, both governmental and private, have expressed continuing concern over the growing number of older persons requiring protective services. Among these are the U.S. Department of Health, Education, and Welfare, the Veterans Administration, the American Bar Foundation, the American Public Welfare Association, the Family Service Association of America, and the National Council on the Aging. In addition, lawyers, physicians, psychiatrists, social workers, psychologists, police officers, bankers, nurses, and others whose work brings them into contact with incapacitated persons are becoming increasingly concerned by the inadequacy of community services and the apparent lack of centralized community responsibility for the welfare of these persons.

Lawyers and social workers, in cooperation with others, can and should make a significant contribution to the alleviation of this problem. Indeed, their participation and cooperation are central to a resolution of the situation confronting many communities and involving increasing numbers of incapacitated persons, especially the aged.

There is much they can do, separately and in concert, to be helpful. For example, greater precision must be sought in distinguishing between professional competence and legal authority, in determining when legal authority and legal sanction should be invoked, in deciding upon whom responsibility shall be placed for acting in behalf of another and in assuring accountability, and in furthering the most constructive use of fiduciary arrangements.

Among the matters requiring continuing attention is the need for doing further research in the psychodynamics of aging; incorporating in law and legal practices and legal institutions new insights derived from increased knowledge in the social and behavioral sciences; eliminating vestiges of criminal law practices in protective services; and exploring further the roles and functions of the guardian, the police officer, the fiduciary, the nurse, the psychologist, and other therapists.

There is also a great need for lawyers, social workers, and others to consider the problems related to the older person whose degree of incapacity or impairment is not such as to warrant involuntary institutionalization or appointment of a legal guardian following a judicial proceeding and determination of legal incompetence, yet whose behavior is such as to warrant some kind of authoritative intervention. This would include, among other possibilities, consideration of relevant factors in respect to use of conservatorship. Consideration should also be given to the feasibility of administrative rather than judicial proceedings and the adaptation and modernization of due process to conform to the unique requirements of incapacitated older adults.

October 1967

6

Lawyer–Social Worker Relationships in the Family Court: Hearing and Disposition

CONCERNED with the relationships of lawyers and social workers in family court matters, the National Conference of Lawyers and Social Workers first addressed the process known as "intake," a step preliminary to legal process.[1] The subject matter of this statement is in logical sequence since it deals with the legal process that follows for those cases progressing beyond the intake process. Further, the necessity of this statement is highlighted by the historic *Gault* decision.[2]

Matters not disposed of at intake or diverted from the legal process are subject to judicial hearings serving one or more of the following purposes:

- To ascertain whether or not the court has jurisdiction of the subject matter and the person.
- To adjudicate the issue after jurisdiction has been established.
- To determine disposition of cases adjudicated.

In addition, hearings may be held to determine the release or predisposition detention of a juvenile or an accused adult. The

---

[1] See pp. 18–22, especially p. 19 and p. 21.

[2] 387 US 1 (1967).

latter hearing may be separate or may be held at the time of another hearing.

Delinquency, neglect, adoption, child custody, matrimonial disputes, paternity proceedings, and actions involving relationships between members of the same family, such as assault on a spouse, nonsupport, desertion, and contributing to the neglect or delinquency of children, are the major family problems dealt with in family court actions. While the full range of these problems may not be consolidated within the jurisdiction of a single family court, a primary goal of the judicial process in these kinds of problems should be to preserve or restore the family as a socially functioning and law-abiding unit of society.

BASIC PRINCIPLES

Whether the action brought in connection with a family matter is of a criminal or civil nature, the following basic principles should guide the relationship of the lawyer and the social worker in whatever court the action is being heard:

1. The family court, or other court dealing with a family problem, is judicial in nature and is governed by rules of evidence, procedure, and due process.

2. The circumstances within the family and the interpersonal relationships of family members may constitute factual evidence necessary to the adjudication of the issue, as well as being pertinent to hearings concerned with detention and the postadjudicative or dispositional process.

3. In promotion of the best interests of the parties and commensurate with the need to respect confidentiality, the lawyer and social worker should share social data concerning the family or its individual members in advance of the hearing. This is especially pertinent to predisposition detention and dispositional hearings in which the information is to be supplied to the court as a guide to making a judicial decision.

4. The goal of preserving or restoring the family as a socially functioning and law-abiding unit is best attained by cooperative efforts of the lawyer and the social worker, by adherence to due process, and by a mutual respect between lawyers and social workers for the areas of competence encompassed by each.

5. Efforts that circumvent due process are reprehensible and promote disrespect for the authority of law and the administration of justice.

ROLE OF THE SOCIAL WORKER

In line with these concepts, the following roles are appropriate:

The primary roles of the social worker in the various types of judicial hearings include acting as a witness to give substantive factual testimony; acting as an expert; performing the professional task of gathering, evaluating, and interpreting social and behavioral data for use by the court; and making recommendations as to predisposition detention or release and as to the final disposition best calculated to solve the presenting problems within the limits established by the statutes. In carrying out these roles, the social worker should:

1. Explore with the defense counsel the resources of the family for coping with the problems at issue to the end that recommendations regarding predisposition detention and the final disposition may be mutually understood if not agreed upon.
2. Work for the resolution of differences of opinion between himself and the lawyer prior to the hearing in court and avoid displays of antagonism or resentment when the differences are opened up in the hearing.
3. Insofar as possible, and in concert with the defense counsel, keep the individual and family informed as to the nature of the upcoming hearing and share with them the recommendations that he plans to make, if any, and the reasons therefor.
4. Obtain the advice and help of legal counsel concerning the validity and pertinence of the factual evidence that he is competent to give and the manner in which this testimony should be given.
5. Present his oral and written information in a well-organized, clear, and concise fashion.
6. Maintain his impartial, professional status in avoiding the role of an advocate.
7. Abstain from furnishing advice or expressing opinions on questions of law.
8. Encourage the individual or family concerned to seek legal counsel.

ROLE OF THE LAWYER

The lawyer representing litigants in family court should:

1. Provide legal advice to his client and represent him at all stages of the proceedings.

2. Participate with the social worker in evaluating circumstances and resources as they may affect detention and final disposition.

3. To the extent permissible under local practice, minimize the adversary nature of the proceedings if, in his judgment, this is appropriate to the effective representation of his client's interests.

4. Share with the social worker the recommendations he believes should be made concerning predisposition detention and the final disposition, in an effort to resolve as many differences as possible before the hearing.

5. Demonstrate appreciation of the role and contribution of the social worker. Reinforce the position of the social worker in carrying out responsibilities that he may have to assume after the hearing on behalf of the lawyer's client.

6. Encourage the social worker to participate in interpreting to the client and family the nature of the proceedings, the functioning of the court, and the reason for the findings of the court.

7. Establish with the client and the social worker the manner and extent to which he will provide postdispositional legal service, if any.

8. Advise the court when, in his estimation, additional counsel is needed for a separate member of the family to avoid a conflict-of-interest situation.

August 1968

7

Confidential and Privileged Communications: Guidelines for Lawyers and Social Workers

CONFIDENTIALITY is a most fundamental and essential element in the relationship between client and social worker and between client and attorney. It is inherent in the social worker–client relationship, in the provision of services by the individualized service agency, and in the advice and representation by the lawyer.

The nondifferentiated use of the terms "confidentiality" and "privileged communication" has been the source of much confusion and misunderstanding in the social work profession. Contributing equally to the misunderstanding between the professions of law and social work is the failure on the part of some lawyers to appreciate the confidential relationship between client and social worker. It is therefore important to distinguish confidentiality from privileged communication. Privileged communications are those confidential communications that are protected from disclosure by law.

Communications between social worker and client, attorney and client, physician and patient, priest and penitent, are made in the confidence or trust that they will not be disclosed to third persons who are not integral and necessary elements of the particular confidential relationship. The confidential nature of these communications is protected by the canons of ethics of the various professions and by the integrity of the professional person to whom the communications are made.

In the law, there are two types of privileged communications, only one of which is related to the discussion of confidentiality and privilege. The only universal privilege is that which attaches to the client for statements made by him to his attorney in the relationship of attorney and client. Because of the balancing of interests between the protection of the individual and the necessity of society to have a complete revelation of the truth, the extension of his privilege has been greatly restricted by the courts, and when extension has taken place, in the main, it has been by legislation. Generally, such protection has been extended to patients in the patient-physician relationship, penitents in the penitent-clergy relationship, and in some states in which social workers have been licensed, the privilege has been extended to their clients as well.

The protection which the privilege affords the client, patient, or penitent is that the professional may not be compelled to testify in any judicial or administrative proceeding as to those confidential communications made within the relationship.

The problem is further complicated for social agencies giving individualized services by reason of the fact that the services they render are supported by the community as a whole, whether through general or special tax revenue or through voluntary contributions. The agency is thus faced with the need to assure the client's right to privacy and, at the same, to account to the public for the manner in which it expends the funds provided by the public. This creates potential conflict in the agency's efforts to perform its functions in a responsible manner. It also creates difficulty for social workers, who by and large practice their profession within and as staff of social agencies, in obtaining the same status of confidentiality as is enjoyed by other professions—in short, the status of privileged communication between social worker and client.

Social services are being made available to more and more people, from all walks of life, and at increasing cost to the public in general. At the same time more and more professional disciplines and auxiliary sources, such as the schools, are becoming involved in the provision of social services in individual cases. Sometimes this leads to different emphases and may involve differences in concept with respect to confidentiality in the sharing of information. Moreover, there is cumulative evidence of increasing concern for the privacy of the individual who seeks and needs the help of social agencies and greater concern on the part of individualized service agencies for safeguarding the concept of confidentiality as one that is basic to the relationship between the client and the social agency.

It is essential therefore to deal with the matter of confidentiality in terms of :

- The social agency's dual responsibility to the client and the public.
- Recognition that the social agency carries responsibility to share, when appropriate, information to facilitate provision of client service.
- Emphasis on the development of the client–social agency relationship and the role of confidentiality in establishing and maintaining that relationship.
- Involvement of the social agency with other agencies, professions, and disciplines in client service.
- Heightened concern for the right of privacy of the individual.
- Acknowledgment that confidentiality, by and large, is not equated with privileged communication.

RECOMMENDATIONS

In view of the foregoing, social agencies providing individualized service should adopt policies in respect to confidentiality that are clear to the worker, the client, and the public. Such policies should undergo periodic review, both in terms of their continuing relevance and effectuation in practice.

In recognition of the rights of individuals seeking assistance from our respective professions and the protection of society, the National Conference of Lawyers and Social Workers recommends to the professions the following principles:

1. Confidentiality assures that disclosures made within the relationship of client and social worker or client and lawyer will be used constructively in the client's behalf and will not be passed on to others except when required by law or when authorized by the client.
2. After the client grants permission to the social worker and the attorney to exchange information or divulge it to the other, each should recognize and respect the trust that the client has placed in the other.
3. Except when there is specific permission from the client, or when authorized or required by law, the social worker should not testify. Nor should the social agency produce its files in any proceeding except when under subpoena or when defending against claims brought by the client against the social worker or agency.
4. When subpoenaed, the social worker or agency should

consult legal counsel as to those matters that are subject to production in court.[1]

5. When records must be produced, every effort should be made to limit demands for information to those matters essential for the purposes of the proceeding.

August 1968

---

1 See p. 8.

8

Interprofessional Relationships at the Graduate School Level: Law and Social Work

THE CONTEMPORARY urban crisis, which was called the greatest "challenge to public order . . . since the Civil War" in the statement "Law and the Changing Society" issued by the American Assembly and the American Bar Association on March 17, 1968, is one of the principal reasons why lawyers and social workers must intensify their collaboration in every way possible.[1] The statement of the American Assembly predicts that the achievement of social justice "will require far-reaching institutional changes." As an example of such change the report states that "our welfare system must do more than support persons in a state of dependency."

The frightening urban crisis and the wide range of skills needed to resolve it point up the tragedy of the almost total isolation of law schools and schools of social work. This isolation is tragic because more and more lawyers and social workers will be handling separate but closely interrelated aspects of the lives of the same persons. It is increasingly self-evident that the major welfare programs of today are based on Federal, State, and local laws and regulations—all of which result in a convergence of work for social

[1] The American Assembly is a national nonpartisan, educational organization, affiliated with Columbia University, which holds nonpartisan meetings and publishes authoritative books to illuminate issues of U.S. policy.

workers and attorneys. Similarly, social workers and lawyers meet in court on an ever more numerous series of matters related to family life, the protection of juveniles, the rights of the aged, and similar issues. The task of breaking down the isolation between law schools and schools of social work may be rendered easier by the ferment and even the revolution in thought about traditional concepts of curriculum that now exist in both law and social work schools.

Because of the urgent need to begin at the earliest possible time that collaboration between lawyers and social workers without which the urban crisis cannot be resolved, the National Conference of Lawyers and Social Workers here sets forth guidelines and principles, along with recommendations, for all schools of law and schools of social work.

GUIDELINES AND PRINCIPLES

In any statement with respect to the reciprocal relationships between lawyers and social workers the following considerations are relevant:

1. It should be candidly acknowledged that legal education and graduate social work education have developed during the past fifty years in substantially different ways. Moreover, mutual ignorance and an unfortunate lack of collaboration between lawyers and social workers have tended to promote a certain alienation if not antagonism between the members of the legal profession and the profession of social work.

2. It should be noted also that there has been an emphasis in legal education on advocacy, which may have overshadowed or de-emphasized the lawyer's role as a counselor and mediator. Similarly, in social work education there may have been a lack of emphasis on the legal rights and responsibilities of persons and an overemphasis on his human needs as a victim of social injustice.

3. It must also be noted that, until very recently, there have been few attempts to bring law and social work students together in a collaborative educational or co-curricular program. The paucity of these attempts is attributable to many factors, some of which may not be identifiable or resolvable. But the central reason for the isolation of law and social work students appears to derive from the assumptions about lawyers and social workers on which professors of law and social work base their curriculum and their method of teaching.

RECOMMENDATIONS

In view of these factors the National Conference of Lawyers and Social Workers makes the following recommendations.

1. Law schools are urged to have material and personnel from the field of social work introduced at all relevant points in the law school curriculum. Knowledge about sound social work principles could usefully be given to law students when they treat the law related to family breakdown, parole, probation, adoption, juvenile delinquency, the commitment of the mentally ill, the rights of the aged and welfare recipients, and a growing number of other subjects. When it is possible, persons skilled in social work—and especially those who are experts in the problems of minority groups—should teach or lecture at law schools.

The National Conference of Lawyers and Social Workers welcomes and encourages the trend by which psychologists, sociologists, and psychiatrists are becoming part-time or full-time members of the faculties of law schools. It is urged that highly qualified social workers be included among those social scientists who are now members of law school faculties. Conversely, schools of social work should have on their faculties attorneys who are knowledgeable about laws affecting those persons or groups whom social workers are being trained to assist.

2. Schools of social work are urged to introduce future social workers to the legal process in a meaningful way so that they may be able to recognize the legal problems of the persons whom they serve. It will be particularly helpful for social work students to understand basic legal institutions and to know about the expanding nature of the guarantees in the Bill of Rights, the recent developments with respect to the constitutional rights of persons in criminal and juvenile cases, and the most progressive thinking about the rights of such persons as public assistance recipients, consumers, and tenants.

Social work students, moreover, will serve their clients more astutely if they learn something of the science of legal investigation and the art of advocacy since this art is utilized by administrative agencies and courts as a means of arriving at the truth. It is particularly important that future social workers be sensitized to the dangers that can result to the persons they seek to serve by anything approaching the unauthorized practice of law.

Basic due process requires that every citizen involved in a contest affecting his liberty, property, or rights be represented by a competent person trained and licensed to practice law under the discipline of the courts. Students in schools of social work must learn to recognize the increasing number of situations in which the complexity of legal issues and even court decisions require that to guard against unjust treatment, a person must be represented by a lawyer qualified to present all legitimate defenses and exhaust all available remedies.

3. It is recommended to the faculties of law schools and schools of social work that, by dialogue and other means, they become ever more aware of their mutuality of interests and the increasing number of matters of common concern to both professions. If a feeling of mutual understanding and trust is to exist between members of the legal profession and members of the social work profession, it would seem that the best way of creating this feeling would be to have it start at the heart of the educational work.

Several methods may be explored to achieve the dialogue that is desirable between students of law and students of social work. Among such methods is a joint enrollment of students in courses of interest to both professions. Perhaps even more fruitful is a working collaboration between students of both professions in a clinical experience in which both groups are exposed to the complexities surrounding the legal rights, responsibilities, and possibilities of those living in poverty.

It is urged that professors from law schools and schools of social work collaborate on a bibliography for students enrolled in universities that do not have both a law school and a school of social work.

The National Conference of Lawyers and Social Workers emphasizes again its central theme and thesis: lawyers and social workers, as close collaborators in situations involving both social and legal problems, should seek to utilize to the full the resources of each profession and to recognize and reconcile their respective professional orientations in order that their joint responsibilities may be faithfully carried out.

June 1969

9

Custody in Matrimonial Proceedings: Lawyer–Social Worker Relationships

In few areas of the law is there a greater need for close co-operation between lawyers and social workers than in matters arising out of matrimonial proceedings that deal with the custody of minors. Existing matrimonial laws and procedures throughout the nation vary considerably, and new proposals are under consideration in many states and by the National Conference of Commissioners on Uniform State Laws, especially as they affect the question of custody. It is not the purpose of this statement to suggest what these laws should be. Rather, it is intended to examine ways in which the professions of law and social work may work together more effectively in helping the courts determine who shall have custody, what visitation shall be allowed, and what additional steps might be taken or proposed for improving the interrelationships of all of the parties to a matrimonial proceeding in respect to the custody of minor children.

GENERAL PROBLEMS RELATING TO CUSTODY

Most writers on the subject of child custody refer to the generally accepted rule that the trial judge shall be guided by "the best interests of the child," but they note that the rule is more often cited than applied. They conclude that there are so many variations and so little uniformity in actual practice that there is an imperative need for providing guides to the courts to help them in the disposition of these matters.

Judges, lawyers, and social workers experienced in this field have suggested that among the basic factors entering into consideration of the question of custody, the following seem to have primary relevance: [1]

1. The interaction and the interrelationships of the parties involved—the child, parent or parents, or any person acting the role of parent.
2. The degree of permanence as a family unit that the existing or proposed home of the child is likely to have.
3. The emotional and economic stability of the existing or proposed home of the child as it may affect the child's emotional and economic needs.
4. The mental and physical health of all the individuals involved.
5. The home, school, and community record and adjustment of the child and the probable effect of a change in custody.
6. The wishes of the child if he is of sufficient age and is capable of forming an intelligent preference.

Among the substantive problems under consideration are these:

1. Should preference generally be given to the mother for children under a given age?
2. Should preference generally be given to parents rather than to a person acting as a parent or to any other third person?
3. Should preference be given to a person acting as a parent rather than to any other third person?
4. What are the pros and cons of divided custody as it may affect the particular child?
5. Under what conditions should visitation be allowed, denied, or modified? Should these be the same in the case of grandparents or other relatives as in the case of the other parent?
6. How often may a parent, or other party without custody, be authorized to seek a change of custody and on what grounds?
7. Should a child be allowed to seek a change of custody or visitation? How often?

---

[1] Some of these are among the factors suggested in a proposed draft of a Uniform Marriage and Divorce Law submitted to the National Conference on Commissioners on Uniform State Laws, and currently under consideration by that body.

8. How can we assure and provide for legal enforcement of custody determinations if and when the child is removed to another state or country?

9. Should a guardian ad litem or attorney for the child be appointed in every case involving questions of custody?

Regardless of what the law is or might be in any given jurisdiction, it seems obvious that in order to assist the court in determining just what will be in the best interests of the child and of justice to all the parties, it becomes essential to utilize fully the abilities of not only the lawyer but also of the social worker or the particular social agency that may be available in the community for this purpose.

ROLE OF THE LAWYER

As in all areas of family life, the lawyer should consider his role not only as a legal advocate for his client but also as a helping professional who may be able to assist his client in arriving at an amicable settlement with the other spouse or relative involved in the custody dispute, without actual resort to the courts. He should see to it that the other spouse or relative is represened by counsel. While it may sometimes be feasible for such a voluntary arrangement to be effected through the intervention of the attorneys alone, more often the hostility between the parties has reached a state that suggests the need for the help of the social work profession. Many lawyers feel it is always advisable to involve a social worker in working out an appropriate and acceptable arrangement for custody and/or visitation. Some do so early in the contact with the family, in planning such arrangements. On the other hand, some attorneys have resisted the use of the social worker because they feel themselves competent in the area. Others are reluctant because they are not aware of the special training and experience of the social worker in dealing with family interrelationships and in being sensitive to some of the latent relevant psychological and emotional factors.

Not all attorneys are equipped by training or experience to do the kind of study that is helpful and essential in arriving at a complete understanding of the underlying motivations in a custody dispute and in arriving at a determination of what is "in the best interests of the child." For example, attempts may be made by one parent to use the child as a pawn in the struggle with the other parent. Sometimes a parent is so interested in punishing the other parent that he does not take into consideration the child's physical or emotional needs. Nor are attorneys always sufficiently skilled so that they can interview the children involved without running the risk of creating even greater trauma than that which may already exist because of the strained relationships in the family group.

There are some lawyers who are gifted enough and trained sufficiently to be able to counsel their own clients in respect to matters of custody and who, in cooperation with equally competent opposing lawyers, can be helpful in arriving at a proper solution; yet most attorneys do not have the capacity or facilities for this important aspect of family counseling, nor do they have the time required for it. Thus, most lawyers might well consider the utilization of a competent social worker or family agency, even prior to court action. Once the court proceeding has been decided upon, there will also be many opportunities for using the skill of the social worker, either in the preparation of the case or during the course of the trial, or both.

In all cases, the lawyer should be aware that what appears to be a sound legal approach—and proper advocacy—needs to be considered in the light of its effect on the child, as well as his parents, and its effect on the possibilities of establishing a tenable interrelationship for the future. In his discussions with the child or the parent, he can benefit from the advice and guidance of the social worker as to the emotional and socioeconomic factors involved. The same rule that guides the court, to wit, "the best interests of the child," must guide the lawyer and the social worker.

A LAWYER FOR THE CHILD

An important issue to consider is whether the concept or rule of the "best interests of the child" is tantamount to a legal right of the child and whether the child should be represented by independent counsel to assure effectuation of that right. It has been suggested by some writers that a child should have a "spokesman" when his own future is being determined, whether or not he himself is old enough to be heard or have his own preferences considered. This might take the form of a guardian ad litem, or attorney, appointed by the court as counsel for the child. Such a lawyer might, after investigation and utilization of the help of a social worker, arrive at an assessment of the needs that should be brought to the court's attention regarding the child's health, personal well-being and education. It has been argued that although each parent is represented by an attorney, neither really speaks for the child or his "best interests," which may, at least in some respects, be antithetical to those of the parents. Is there not, then, a need for independent representation of the child?

ROLE OF THE SOCIAL WORKER

The social worker may become involved in a child custody proceeding in one of many ways. He may be a staff member of the court or its probation service. He may be a private practitioner or a staff member of a family or children's agency, which has been called in for assistance or to which the family has already become known through past contacts.

The social worker should be aware of the legal implications in the situation and should rely on the lawyer for such information and guidance. He must not attempt to give legal advice, regardless of his years of experience in the field. Nor should he suggest a course of conduct for the parties without consultation with the attorneys involved. It is possible that what appears to be a sound casework approach could have a serious effect on the legal proceeding.

The social worker needs to recognize that he is functioning in an adversary system. This may create the need for compromising in a way that, at first glance, may not seem to be consistent with the best possible social approach.

The social worker may be of assistance to the lawyer in advising when children should be interviewed and, when interviewing is necessary, whether they should be questioned in the lawyer's office, in open court, or in chambers. It is important not to exacerbate further the already existing fears and hostilities. Thus he should make available to the attorney with whom he is cooperating whatever social and psychological data he is privileged to share. Some lawyers have a social worker present at any interview with the child and with the parent.

In reporting to the court the social worker is of course bound by the laws and rules of the courts in the particular jurisdiction. In some states such reports are confidential, to be disclosed to the parties and/or the attorneys only with the express permission of the court. Other states have held that unless there has been a consent or waiver to the contrary by the parties, all reports to the court must be disclosed to the parties and/or the attorneys, and the reporting social worker is subject to cross-examination. It has been suggested that in every court proceeding affecting custody, contested or uncontested, there should be a court-appointed or staff social worker to investigate and report. It seems appropriate that such report and recommendations should be shared with the parties and counsel, subject to cross-examination. Although some feel that such investigations should be required only when the question of custody is actually at issue, others propose that an appropriate study and report would be helpful in every custody matter, since sometimes proposed agreements are not in the "best interests of the child" and often are based more on the pressures of arriving at a settlement than on a careful evaluation of how the child's life is being affected.

FOR BOTH PROFESSIONS

Reference has been made to the conflict of laws and to the impermanence of custody determinations arising not out of altered circumstances but rather because of jurisdictional factors. Only too frequently, a disappointed spouse will establish a new residence—real or otherwise—for the express purpose of seeking to overturn a custody decision by appealing to the courts of another state. The effect of a new and different determination on the child whose well-being is at stake and whose best interests are supposed to be of central importance is frequently not considered. Nor is consideration given to the capacity of the court to make an appropriate study of the potential impact of a drastic change on the child.

Permanence and stability are of utmost importance to a minor child whose life has already been scarred by the trauma of parental conflict and marital discord. If "the best interests of the child" is to be more than an empty phrase, lawyers and social workers must join in study and demonstration of the effect of jurisdictional conflicts on the lives of children in custody, and appropriate measures must be sought to remedy this situation.

Further study is indicated with respect to providing for continuing jurisdiction of the court in supervising the custodial relationship that is established. Should the court or its representative have the responsibility for and the right to extended supervision of the effectiveness of the arrangement and the adequacy with which the terms of the order are being carried out? Should the child, on his own initiative, be allowed to raise questions about the effectiveness of the plan or about specific details—such as visitation, schooling, traveling, and the like—in the same way that the parents or other parties to the proceeding do?

In any event, it is clear that responsible disposition of questions related to custody will call upon the highest skill of both the lawyer and the social worker and that cooperation between these two professional disciplines is indispensable to the appropriate resolution of the serious problems involved.

January 1970

Appendix

The National Conference of Lawyers and Social Workers

Since the National Conference of Lawyers and Social Workers is the offspring of the Section of Family Law of the American Bar Association (ABA), it behooves the Conference to make a periodic accounting of its activities to its parent body. A parent ought to evaluate its child objectively, if possible, and hopefully constructively. Initially, this parent appropriately kept a tight rein on this child, but the child has matured and gained a measure of independence. Primarily, this independence has been financial, so it has been welcomed. Otherwise, however, it is important that the relationship remain close and cordial and that problems and concerns be shared.

The Conference is not a conference in the usual sense of the word. Its name derives from its fellow conferences that were organized by the ABA and several professional and business groups to reduce tensions and eliminate unauthorized practice of law. Indeed, this Conference is answerable to the standing Committee on the Unauthorized Practice of Law as well as to the Section of

---

This is an abbreviated version of a fifth-year accounting of the work of the National Conference of Lawyers and Social Workers that was written by a former Co-Chairman for the American Bar Association. It reviews the objectives of the group and the accomplishments from its formation in 1962 through 1967.—Ed.

Family Law and has had at all times at least one member of that committee on its roster.

The Conference was authorized in 1962 by the Board of Governors of the ABA. The President issued an invitation to the National Association of Social Workers (NASW) to form the Conference for the following purposes:

1. To draft statements of principles defining the legitimate activities of social workers and lawyers in those areas in which each have a vital interest. Such statements would be submitted to the parent organizations for approval. They would be separated into the various areas of concern: for example, adoptions, marriage counseling, juvenile delinquency, court employees, and so forth.

2. To prevent the unauthorized practice of law by defining those areas in family law that are within the competence only of lawyers and to receive, analyze, and dispose of complaints arising in this area. It was hoped that the National Conference would serve as an advisory body to those, whether lawyers, judges, or social workers, who contemplated projects that might infringe on the practice of law.

3. To serve as a clearinghouse for the interests of social welfare agencies and/or legal groups in the development of legislation by disseminating activities in this area from each group to the other and by suggesting the areas in which each group ought to be consulted.

4. To gather and disseminate information concerning research projects in order to prevent duplication of effort and to make available to all interested groups the information thus acquired.

5. To do everything possible to promote a better understanding between lawyers and social workers without, however, committing the parent organizations to any particular activity without their prior consent.

The Conference is composed of sixteen members with co-chairmen. Eight are appointed by the president of the ABA and eight by the Board of Directors of NASW. The terms of the members have been staggered so that continuity will be preserved. There has always been a close association with the Section of Family Law by way of membership.

There can be little doubt that the potential of this Conference for producing a better rapport between lawyers and social workers has caught the fancy of many individuals. Both lawyers and social workers have seen the need for this activity in our rapidly changing society and have materially demonstrated their interest and concern.

The efforts of the Conference have been devoted largely to three activities: the development of statements of principles in areas of mutual concern to social workers and lawyers, the stimulation of conferences in communities between lawyers and social workers, and the exploration of ways and means—through foundation grants and other resources—to make a more significant impact in the first two areas and in those that have of necessity been left largely unexplored.

PUBLICATION OF STATEMENTS

The most satisfying accomplishment of the Conference has been the publication of four statements and the promise of further statements. The published statements have appeared in the *Family Law Quarterly*. It is gratifying that thousands of these documents have been distributed upon request both to bar associations and to social welfare groups and agencies. Well over 10,000 copies of the "Rights of Public Assistance Recipients" and over 5,000 of the "Family Court Intake" publications have been distributed and more copies are being requested.

Moreover, the U.S. Department of Health, Education, and Welfare has distributed the statement on "Rights of Public Assistance Recipients" widely throughout the country, including distribution to every state and county welfare department, their administrators, board members, and key staff.

In order for any document to be published by the Conference, it must first be approved by the Council of the Section of Family Law, by the Standing Committee on Unauthorized Practice of Law, by either the Board of Governors or the House of Delegates of the ABA and by the Board of Directors of NASW. This process may require as much as a year and rarely has taken less than six months, since the various divisions of the ABA meet simultaneously and thus it is not practicable to move from one to another at the same meeting time. It must also be kept in mind that before any statement is submitted to any approving body, it is subjected to the caldron of the Conference itself. Every line—indeed, almost every word—is discussed and debated. Each statement has gone through many drafts. For example, there were eight drafts of the statement on "Lawyer–Social Worker Relationships in the Family Court Intake Process."

The drafting of each statement has revealed, even among the sophisticated members of the Conference, many areas that require clarification, much lack of full understanding of respective roles and goals. Discussion does not always resolve these differences entirely, but it does enlarge the vision and produce modifications of established viewpoints. It is an exciting experience to seek and find resolutions to differing concepts and attitudes. These resolutions do not require a compromise of principles but rather a recognition of the essential differences in competence and service, which when properly used, can be made to work together for the greater benefit of the public. It is fondly to be hoped that the education of the Conference members through this process has an effect beyond the Conference on the professional attitudes of their respective colleagues throughout the country.

Every lawyer knows that the most difficult part of draftsmanship is the production of the first draft. It has been so with these documents and grateful credit should be paid to the men who have labored over these first drafts and assumed continuing responsibility for them. For example, Louis L. Bennett wrote the draft of the statement on the "Rights of Public Assistance Recipients." It is a unique document and bears the imprint of his wealth of experience and extraordinary ability to write with clarity both as a lawyer and a social worker, for he is both. Any amendments that were made to the document by the Conference did not detract from the contribution made by Mr. Bennett in conceiving and producing the initial statement. So, too, did Willis Thomas labor long and patiently over the statement on "Family Court Intake Process." This statement required much discussion to clarify concepts and the meaning of certain terminology. The statement entitled "Adult Protective Services—Responsibilities and Reciprocal Relationships of the Lawyer and Social Worker" was prepared by Louis L. Bennett in collaboration with Karl Zukerman, son of Judge Zukerman, and lawyer on the staff of the Community Service Society of New York. The statement on "Confidential and Privileged Communications" was prepared by Carl Ingraham. Each of these statements involves unique legal and social problems and each raises fundamental questions of practice and policy. The resolution of these questions is imperative if law and social work are to function effectively in the new institutions being created for the resolution of family problems and the protection of private and public interests.

Many basic differences between lawyers and social workers are raised in the production of these statements. For example, unauthorized practice of law in the field of family law is as ill defined and as poorly understood as it is in most other areas. Lawyers as well as others who are reluctant to face this problem frankly would be well advised to heed the statements of President Orison S. Marden quoted in an editorial in the *American Bar Association Journal,* Volume 53, page 726:

> At the institute we have referred to, President Marden gave an opening address. Among other things, he said "The lawyer who thinks that unauthorized practice work is simply a means for increasing his own income has no place in this discussion."
>
> He reminded the institute that we believe the correct functioning of our society "requires a system of courts and lawyers to resolve justiciable disputes between the citizens and between the citizen and government." This in turn requires that we have "judges and lawyers, specially educated, continuously trained, admitted to practice by specific license and subject to stern standards of conduct." Without these, "our liberties and our way of life would be in jeopardy." It is, therefore, in the interest of our entire society that lawyers alone be licensed to practice law, and this gives paramount importance to the line of demarcation between lawyers and others whose work touches on the practice of law.
>
> We cannot overemphasize the message President Marden brought to the institute. As he said, "Our concern in this subject matter is governed by broad consideration of social policy and the public interest. It must not be motivated by selfishness, by competition for competition's sake, or by avaricious materialism."

CHANGING CLIMATE

To produce a climate that reflects President Marden's admonitions is one of the chief functions of the Conference. It has been apparent to some for many years that a lack of cordiality between lawyers and social workers grew out of a lack of understanding and appreciation of the nature of the service that each was trained and competent to perform. When lawyers attempt to practice social work and social workers attempt to practice law, it is largely because neither fully appreciates the dimensions of the other's profession. Whenever lawyers and social workers are required, the results are immeasurably enhanced if they work together with conviction and are seriously retarded if they fail to do so. It has been demonstrated time and again, both nationally and locally, that there is no basic incompatibility between these two groups and that they can readily reach accord once they sit down together to counsel with each other. The Conference is itself one example of cooperation that has produced significant results.

It has always been understood that any permanent impact on lawyer–social worker relationships must occur at the community level. No matter how widespread the Conference's activities may become, they cannot replace local conferences. While there are many similarities among communities, there are also regional and sectional differences. But bar associations and chapters of NASW exist in all major communities, and many have already initiated joint meetings. All that is really required to establish such conferences is initiative on the part of a few individuals, with some help and stimulation from the national organizations. Ralph H. Logan, a member of the Conference, has devoted many hours to correspondence with many bar associations on this matter. He has had many encouraging responses, but he and the Conference recognize that a much greater effort must be made to serve such interest and to arouse more intelligent concern if lasting results are to be obtained. This cannot be accomplished alone by one busy practicing lawyer no matter how devoted he is. A far more effective organization for the effort is required if a real impact on law and social welfare is to be made.

This experience with local bar associations, as well as the general interest in its work that the Conference has stimulated, has caused the Conference to ponder its future. It is obvious that since it was founded a greatly increased demand has arisen for improved cooperation between law and social work. The whole development of legal services for the poor has burgeoned in this period under the Office of Economic Opportunity, the activities of which have also enormously affected many urban relationships. No amount of slowdown or so-called backlash will appreciably affect the thrust of this movement to eradicate poverty, to improve the condition and character of urban life, and to endow the human rights promised by democracy with consequential substance. The American Bar Association has boldly aligned itself with these purposes and so, too, has every organization of and for social workers. It is obvious that this social upheaval has and will continue to challenge both lawyers and social workers to think anew and to perform anew. The Conference, organized for the specific purpose of providing a meaningful forum for lawyers and social workers, finds itself somewhat frustrated in its desire to serve adequately in these challenging times.

In an effort to look forward to the fulfillment of its purposes, the Conference has been studying ways and means for improving its productivity. Some years ago the Department of Labor stated that the professions of law and social work were the least productive of all professions. Lawyers have been concerned with this aspect of their profession, and many articles have been written to encourage lawyers to become more productive. The ponderous, almost pachydermous, movement of the Conference is an unhappy example of this condition. No staff aids in research for a draft of the statements. There are no funds for supplying the kind of continuous housekeeping that maintains an orderly and enthusiastic control over the activities of any complex organization. All of the work is done by people already overburdened with their primary professional and other extracurricular activities. "Thought" personnel must also be "productive" personnel. This is not efficient and will inevitably produce too little too late.

Recognizing these facts, the Conference has called upon the staff of the American Bar Foundation and especially its executive director, Geoffrey Hazard, to help explore its future and the future of its problems. Several meaningful discussions have been held. There is a consensus that among the issues with which the Conference wrestles and which are arising out of the changing patterns of our society, there are many that ought to be studied in depth. It is hoped that these can be isolated and that the Foundation will accept some of them for research. This would undergird the Conference's work with some answers to some of the basic problems. In no area more than this one are there so many assumptions, the validity of which has yet to be confirmed.

Several essential areas lie largely unexplored by the Conference. It is hoped that a significant study can be made that looks toward improving the relations of and contacts between law schools and schools of social work. This area has been much discussed by the Conference, but with little opportunity to move forward. So too the *Gault* decision (*Re Gault*, 18 L. ed. 2d, 527) has produced new questions for exploration by the Conference.

Whitney North Seymour, former President of the American Bar Association, once told the author of this report, when he was chairman of the Section of Family Law, that the Section was the conscience of the Bar. It was men like Seymour who awakened the conscience of the Bar in many areas, and since then every President of the American Bar Association has been acutely concerned that the Bar shall fulfill its historic role in this area of social concern. The Conference is only one expression of this activity.

It has developed a technique for producing a better climate within which lawyers and social workers can more effectively serve the public together.

In conclusion, it should be noted that Conferences are people, and people produce results. If this Conference has succeeded, it is because of the people who believed in it and have devoted their time to it. Paramount among these is Jacob T. Zukerman. Before being elevated to the court, he was the co-chairman for NASW. He was far more than that. He was the secretary, the guardian, and the support of the Conference. Without his unstinting efforts, it would not have been viable. When the author of this article was president of the National Conference of Social Welfare and called upon the members of the Conference, and especially Mr. Zukerman, to help him develop a program on law and social welfare, it was Mr. Zukerman who took nebulous ideas and breathed life into them. This is what the Conference is still doing and will continue to do as long as dedicated men like Judge Zukerman devote their time and talent to its activities. Every person who has been or is a member of the Conference will attest that the association of members with each other has made it all more than worthwhile.

by Sol Morton Isaac

December 1967

7/73—2M—L&SW